INSIDE OUT YOGA

SANDRA K
&
JOANNE DE SIMONE

ILLUSTRATED BY ANNETTE LEE

Moonlight Garden
Publications

Renton, Washington

Cover art and illustrations by Annette Lee.
Edited by Caitlyn M. Schmidt.

978-1-938281-84-6   (paperback)
978-1-938281-85-3   (e-book)

Library of Congress Control Number: 2020925946

Published 2021, Moonlight Garden Publications,
an imprint of Gazebo Gardens Publishing, LLC,
Renton, Washington
www.GazeboGardensPublishing.com

Printed in the United States of America.

To my beloved mother and father,
Joyce and Sidney Roth

—SANDRA K

To my brilliant brother,
Richard

—JOANNE DE SIMONE

REVIEWS FOR *INSIDE OUT YOGA*

"*Inside Out Yoga* Offers Roadmap to Inner Peace"

"In this time of incredible tension and uncertainty, we need an outlet to release our built-up stress now more than ever, and in one short month, a local author will provide a new way to accomplish this vital need with the release of the book *Inside Out Yoga*. Water Mill resident Sandra K and co-author Joanne de Simone have created a roadmap to inner peace in a tome filled with more than 30 yoga poses and techniques that guide readers through the simple act of breathing, to the more advanced headstand pose, and a lesson in the seven chakras.

"Each chapter comprises an illustration demonstrating a yoga pose, a few lines to describe the stance's purpose, and a space for self-reflection, where readers can write down the thoughts and feelings experienced while engaged in the pose. Annette Lee's illustrations of strong, serene women, brings a sense of power and body-positivity to readers, while the accompanying description offers a promise of increased wellbeing—from the Fish Pose's, 'Take comfort, disease dissipates,' to the Tortoise Pose's, 'Quell insomnia, awake refreshed.'

"The following lines read like a stanza of poetry, both describing how to perform the stance and its effect on the mind, body, and soul. Those uninitiated in the art of yoga and experts alike can expect to be overcome with peace and confidence when reading each carefully worded, uplifting line. Finally, the blank space for self-reflection offers the chance for readers to look deep into their soul and locate the tranquility, bliss, and mindfulness that have been buried there under life's countless stressors.

"At the end of the reader's journey, they're tasked with taking the insights and feelings unearthed to create a vision board of words, photos, and drawings that illustrate their inner desires and dreams for this life. *Inside Out Yoga* offers its readers a level of inner peace unthinkable in today's stressful world, as well as the guide necessary to maintain that serenity and wellbeing through whatever life throws at us next."

—David Taylor, *Dan's Papers — This is the Hamptons!*
www.danspapers.com

"For the many folks who wish they had found yoga in their youth, *Inside Out* is a must for beginners of all ages to understand how to influence their bodies in a positive way—beautifully written and illustrated, allowing easy access to age-old practices."

—*Lienette Crafoord,*
Hamptons Hot Yoga
www.hamptonshotyoga.com

"Enjoyed the book and how the chosen iconic poses were illustrated, keeping the posture active...loved scholastic tight 'workbook' format, text and illustrations...simple and efficient...accommodates all levels of the yoga asana practice...abundance of playfulness...appealing to all ages."

—*Jimmy Minardi,*
Wellness and Fitness Coach
www.minarditraining.com

"A straightforward, comprehensive look at vital aspects of wellness, connecting chakras and yoga concepts, introducing powerful ancient principles, with a personal Vision Board to chart a mindful course to well-being and wholeness."

—*Leandro Carvalho,*
Creator of Brazil Butt Lift and YouV2,
renowned Beachbody Master,
Fitness Trainer, and Wellness Expert at
Mountainside Treatment Center
www.leandrofitness.com

TABLE OF CONTENTS

INTRODUCTION

As with any path to discovery,

All begins from within...

Our bodies, our minds, our spirit,

Alive with inner beauty...

Ready to find the way out as a great light,

Creating harmony and the blissful connection

To nature and a gracious universe...

"*As above, is below, as within,
so without, as the universe, so the soul...*"

—HERMES TRISMEGISTUS

THE BREATH

Nature's power is as close as our breath

Breathing is the bridge
Between the mind and body...
As through your nose to circulate
The flow of oxygen,
Allow past inner thoughts
To fade and make way
For greater clarity and freedom
To embrace your true essence...

THE BREATH: *I FEEL THE LIFE ESSENCE...*

OM

THE SOUND OF THE UNIVERSE

Say it aloud, or whisper it low,
The sound of creation, divine echo...
"Aum" - "Aum" - "Aum"
The chant before and after practice...
Tuning into its sound of silence
And the embodiment of nature,
Feel the calming movement
As you connect with a world
Of inner peace and sanctity...

OM: *I FEEL THE VIBRATION...*

_____

_____

_____

_____

_____

_____

_____

_____

_____

_____

_____

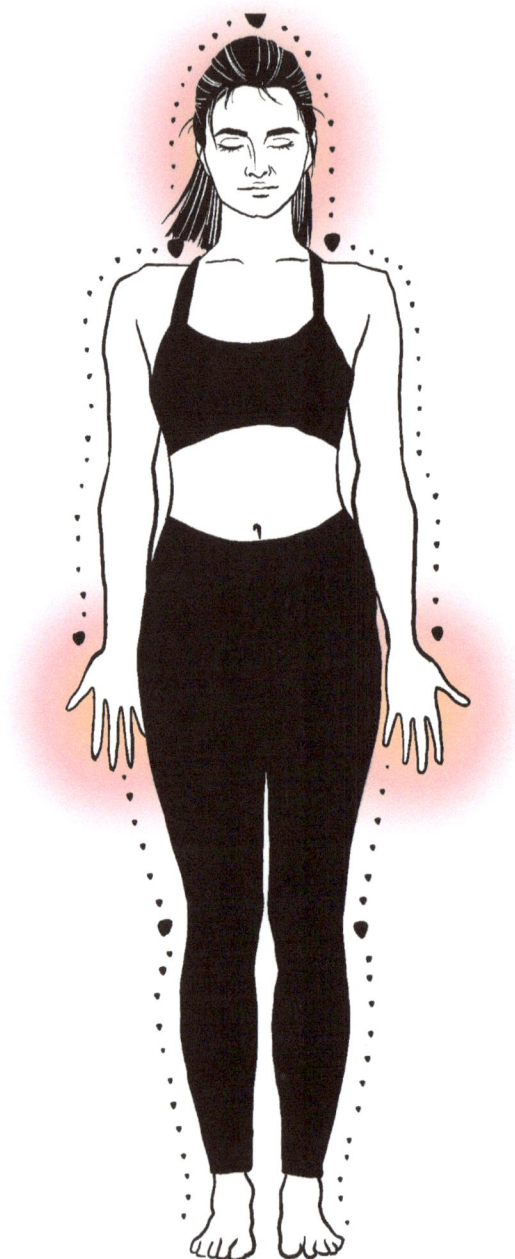

MOUNTAIN POSE

Be PRESENT, GROUNDED, CALM

Like a mountain, you are strong,
Grounded, tall, standing unshakable...
Always planted in the present,
Focused, balanced, calm, and connected...

MOUNTAIN POSE: *I FEEL THE STRENGTH...*

_____

_____

_____

_____

_____

_____

_____

_____

_____

_____

_____

_____

_____

_____

_____

_____

TREE POSE

Grounded in balance, stretch to the sky

Steady and sturdy the tree stands...
Strong roots, flexible branches
To extend and relax your mind,
Providing stability to your legs
And your entire body...

TREE POSE: *I FEEL THE STABILITY...*

_____

_____

_____

_____

_____

_____

_____

_____

_____

_____

_____

_____

_____

_____

_____

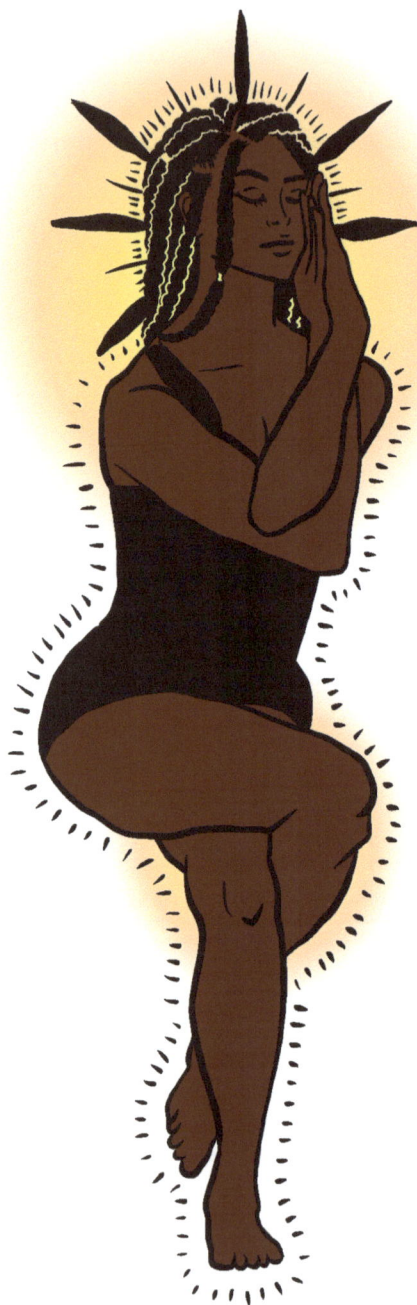

EAGLE POSE

SOAR TO THE LIMITLESS HEAVENS

When the eagle's wings are closed,
It concentrates, feels protected,
Then takes to the open air...
Unfolding, stretching, majestic,
Confident in its kingly flight,
Gliding calmly with poise and serenity...

EAGLE POSE: *I FEEL THE CONFIDENCE...*

DOWNWARD FACING DOG POSE

CONNECT TO YOUR CENTER, CONNECT TO THE WORLD

Release your body's tension and stress,
Elongate your spine evenly, decrease pain...
Strengthen your hands and feel your chest open
To receive fresh oxygen to your head
As your inner glow radiates to the outside world...

DOWNWARD FACING DOG POSE:
I FEEL THE CONNECTION...

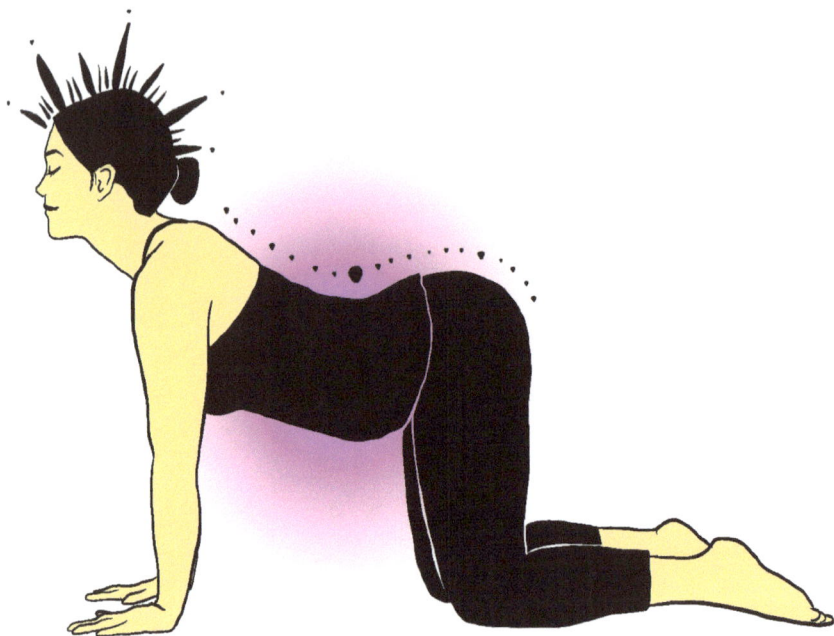

CAT-COW POSE

CREATURES RELAXED IN NATURE'S EMBRACE

Eliminate tension in your neck and upper back...
Open your chest and lungs
For easy breathing to promote relaxation...
Increase coordination, improve posture,
Create the calm of emotional balance...

CAT-COW POSE: *I FEEL THE RELAXATION...*

_____

_____

_____

_____

_____

_____

_____

_____

_____

_____

_____

_____

_____

_____

UPWARD FACING DOG POSE

An open heart feels safe and secure

Build confidence as you eliminate worry
While you stretch your abdomen
And stimulate organs to relieve fatigue...
Strengthen your spine...
Open your chest and heart
To let calm reside within...

UPWARD FACING DOG POSE:
I FEEL CALM WITHIN...

COBRA POSE

A FLEXIBLE FRAME, A FIRM DERRIERE

Your mood is elevated as your body
Finds more flexibility and a stronger spine...
Stimulate digestive organs, strengthen lungs,
Lengthen your neck and shoulders,
And your heart will be open to joy...

COBRA POSE: *I FEEL THE HEART AWAKENED...*

_____
_____
_____
_____
_____
_____
_____
_____
_____
_____
_____
_____
_____
_____
_____

CROW POSE

FEELINGS, EMOTIONS, CREATIVITY CONVERGE

Your arms and wrists will discover
Their strength improved and invigorated...
Your core builds endurance, balance, and focus,
Your upper back stretched,
Poised to release the creator in you...

CROW POSE: *I FEEL THE ENDURANCE...*

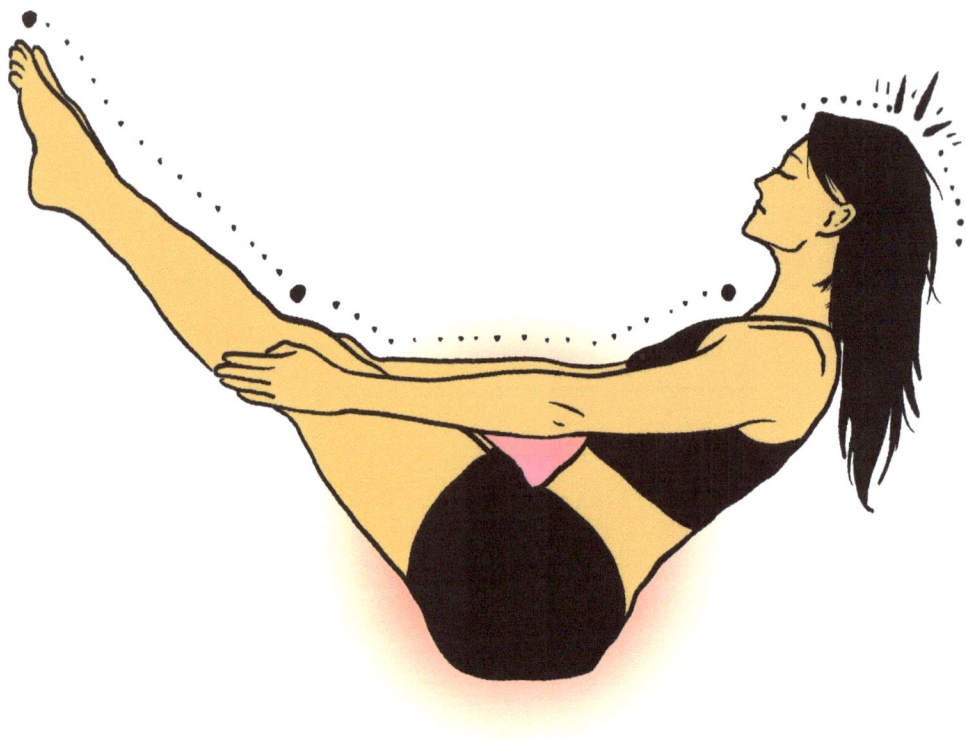

BOAT POSE

BETTER DIGESTION, SMOOTHER SAILING

As your stress is released,
Your core builds better posture...
Improving your breathing,
Your focus is fortified...
Spine and hip flexors strengthened,
Abdominal muscles toned, digestion improved,
Your confidence is increased...

BOAT POSE: *I FEEL THE SUPPORT...*

CHAIR POSE

STRONG MUSCLES, GENERAL GOOD HEALTH

Stimulate your circulation
And your metabolic system...
As all your muscles feel stronger,
Tone your shoulders, hips, bottom,
Your thighs and ankles, too,
For an overall sense of well-being...

CHAIR POSE: *I FEEL THE FOCUS...*

_____

_____

_____

_____

_____

_____

_____

_____

_____

_____

_____

_____

_____

BRIDGE POSE

*B*YE-BYE BLUES, RENEW ON A PIER OF PEACE

Relieve anxiety, revive your energy,
Strengthen your neck and spine...
Serenity fills your nervous system
As stress is alleviated
And replaced with blissful calm...

BRIDGE POSE: *I FEEL THE STILLNESS...*

WHEEL POSE

The Great Inversion, Heart Above Head

When you stretch your entire body,
Your spine is fully flexed...
Thyroid and pituitary glands are energized,
Hormones balance to aid fertility...
Open your heart for the love light to shine...

WHEEL POSE: *I FEEL THE LOVE...*

_____

_____

_____

_____

_____

_____

_____

_____

_____

_____

_____

_____

_____

_____

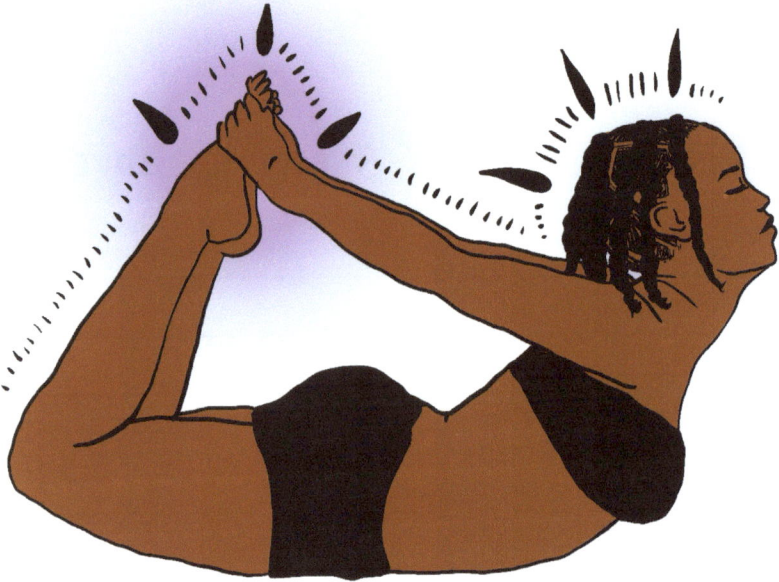

BOW POSE

Meet new challenges with confidence

Aiming high like the archer's bow,
Stretch beyond your comfort level...
See progress in weight loss and better digestion...
Improve posture and stand upright
As hip and abdominal muscles extend...
Your choices radiate self-reliance...

BOW POSE: *I FEEL THE SELF-RELIANCE...*

TRIANGLE POSE

EMOTIONS IN CONTROL, FOCUS TIGHTENED

Open the sides of your waist and hips...
Relieve stress, manage menstrual cycles...
Stimulate organs, improve metabolism,
Tone your knees and ankles,
Stretch your legs and groin...
Graceful, balanced, and brave...

TRIANGLE POSE: *I FEEL THE BRAVERY...*

DANCER POSE

A *CLEAR MIND ENCOUNTERS AN AWAKENED SPIRIT*

Stretch your shoulders and chest,
Open your ribcage,
Bring more air into your lungs...
Improve balance, build strength,
Challenge your mind and body
For concentration, focus, and discipline...

DANCER POSE: *I FEEL THE CONCENTRATION...*

_____

_____

_____

_____

_____

_____

_____

_____

_____

_____

_____

_____

_____

WARRIOR ONE POSE

FUEL MUSCLES TO GO THE DISTANCE

Develop balance, energize your body...
From your strong core, become a force...
With stamina, you become grounded...
Tone your shoulders, arms, legs, and back,
Support circulation, respiration, and concentration...
The challenge becomes a melted candle...

WARRIOR ONE POSE:
I FEEL THE FORCE...

PEACEFUL WARRIOR POSE

BALANCE WITH PEACE, EMBRACE THE STORM

Open your hips and elongate your spine
In a full body stretch, calming your nerves...
Feel the absence of strife, your balance improved...
Fortify core muscles and boost self-esteem,
Shielded by an inner armor,
Balanced and stable with tranquility...

PEACEFUL WARRIOR POSE:
I FEEL THE PROTECTION...

CHILD POSE

Feel safe, peaceful, blissful

With your spine naturally curved
Like a babe nestled in the womb,
Oxygen circulates throughout the body...
Tension relieved, enveloped in calm,
A resting posture to invite peace,
Your body and mind in perfect harmony...

CHILD POSE: *I FEEL THE SERENITY...*

FISH POSE

Take comfort, disease dissipates

Metabolism heightened, energy up...
Stimulate belly organs, regulate hormones,
Tone front of neck and abdominals,
Feel spinal flexibility and upper back stretch...
Be reassured with a better emotional outlook...

FISH POSE: *I FEEL THE FLEXIBILITY...*

_____

_____

_____

_____

_____

_____

_____

_____

_____

_____

_____

_____

_____

_____

_____

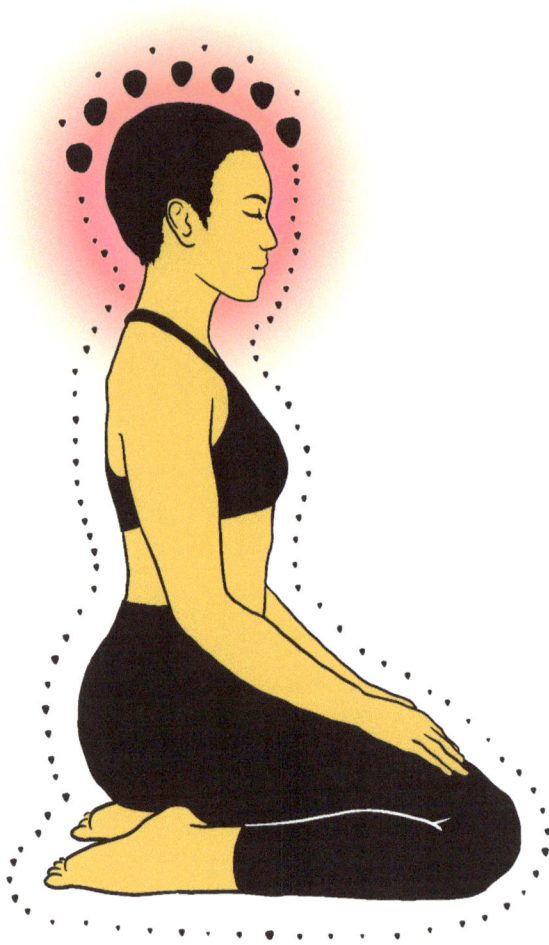

HERO POSE

The world is outside, transform from within

Relieve inner anxiety with quiet meditation...
Strengthen foot arch, improve digestion,
Gain better circulation in your legs,
Assist in asthma relief, and lower blood pressure...
In stillness, realize the victory...

HERO POSE: *I FEEL THE VICTORY...*

_____

_____

_____

_____

_____

_____

_____

_____

_____

_____

_____

_____

_____

_____

RABBIT POSE

MINDFUL OF THE BODY, SERENE IN MIND

Breathe to increase body awareness,
Calm your mind for better sleep...
Increase blood flow to your head,
Decrease and dissolve mental woes,
Stimulate metabolism and digestion...
Bring body and mind in sync, spirit lightened...

RABBIT POSE: *I FEEL THE AWARENESS...*

_____

_____

_____

_____

_____

_____

_____

_____

_____

_____

_____

_____

_____

TORTOISE POSE

QUELL INSOMNIA, AWAKE REFRESHED

Abdomen poised, awareness of breathing...
A limber lower back, elongated spine,
Blood circulates freely, activating muscles,
Kind to your liver and kidneys...
Fill lungs with oxygen, reduce allergies...
Inner thoughts thrive with confidence...

TORTOISE POSE: *I FEEL THE TRANQUILITY...*

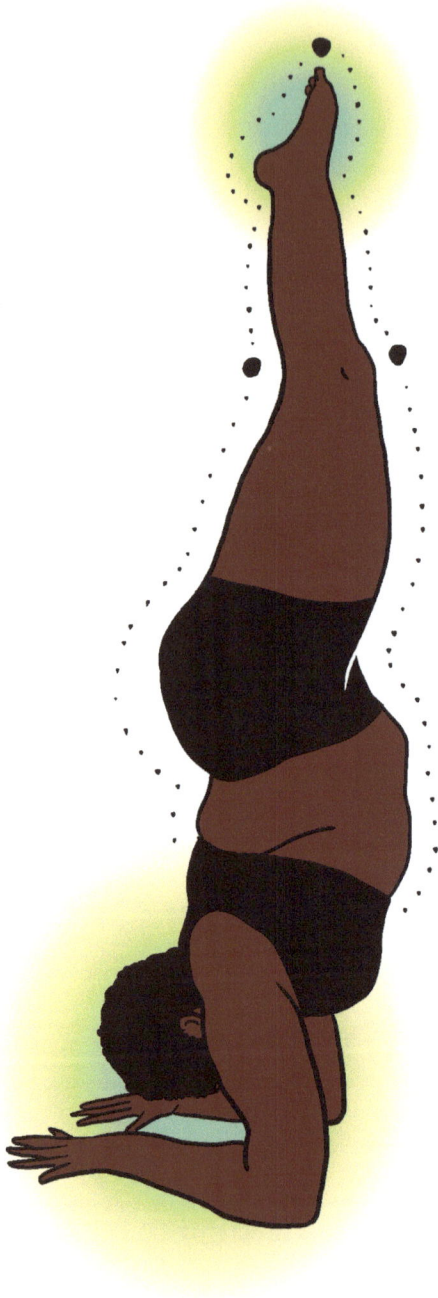

HEADSTAND POSE

Upside down, wear the crown

With increased blood flow to your scalp,
Strengthen your body, build stamina...
Stress hormones are flushed and balanced...
Feel full muscle vitality to your core...
Body inverted, feel awakened in spirit,
Fortified by the "King" of all asanas...

HEADSTAND POSE: *I FEEL THE RENEWAL...*

_____

_____

_____

_____

_____

_____

_____

_____

_____

_____

_____

_____

_____

CAMEL POSE

Create new possibilities, awaken the heart

Posture improved, abdominals expanded,
A more flexible spine, toned and elongated thighs...
With emotional release, surrender and let go,
Heal and balance chakras for caring and compassion...

CAMEL POSE: *I FEEL THE RELEASE...*

_____

_____

_____

_____

_____

_____

_____

_____

_____

_____

_____

_____

_____

_____

_____

_____

MALASANA POSE

ENERGIZED AND GROUNDED IN THE GARLAND OF JOY

Healthier hips and pelvis, increase mobility,
Regulate your sexual energy,
Improve your balance and concentration,
Relax your internal organs...
Positive thoughts become treasured pearls...

MALASANA POSE: *I feel the bliss...*

_____

_____

_____

_____

_____

_____

_____

_____

_____

_____

_____

_____

_____

_____

_____

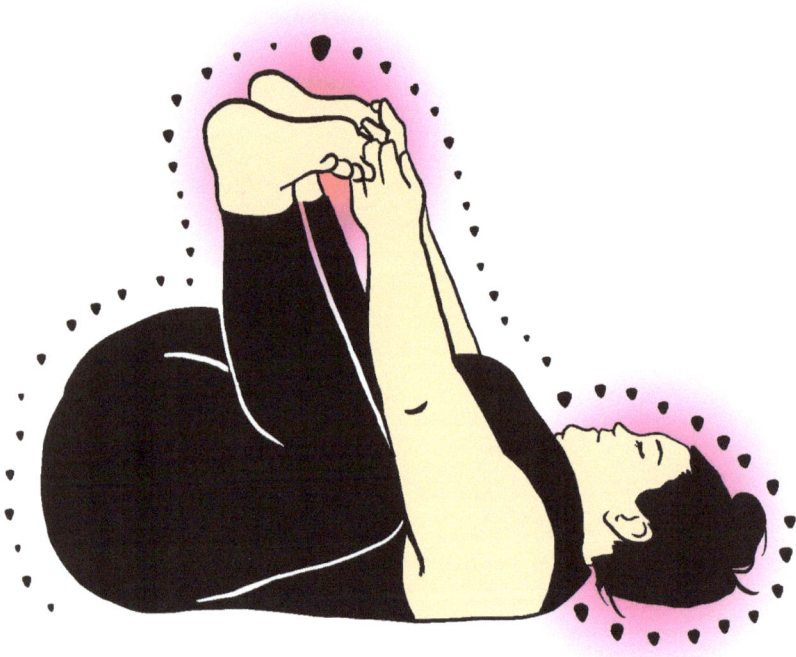

HAPPY BABY POSE
FEELING SECURE KNOWING WHERE YOU BELONG

Intuition heightened, female sexuality enlightened,
Calm your brain, breathe deeply,
Relieve stress and fatigue, increase blood circulation...
Gently stretch your inner groin and spine,
Relax internal organs, support metabolism...
Be playful with childlike energy...

HAPPY BABY POSE:

I FEEL THE PLAYFULNESS...

_____

_____

_____

_____

_____

_____

_____

_____

_____

_____

_____

_____

_____

LOTUS POSE

From a robust root, a flower blossoms

Open your hips to release impulsive unease...
Enhance your physical and emotional well-being,
Connect to your center, embrace the world outside...
A balanced root chakra, grounded in happiness,
A perfect connection of mind, body, and spirit...

LOTUS POSE: *I FEEL THE PEACE...*

_____
_____
_____
_____
_____
_____
_____
_____
_____
_____
_____
_____
_____
_____
_____
_____

UJJAYI PRANAYAMA

Breathe, breathe, balance life energy

Control your breath one nostril at a time...
With awareness, alternate inhaling and exhaling...
Release toxins, normalize heart rate,
Boost your immune system, stabilize your mood...
Be in the moment, discover true mindfulness...
The past and the future are floating feathers...

UJJAYI PRANAYAMA:
I FEEL THE MINDFULNESS...

_____

_____

_____

_____

_____

_____

_____

_____

_____

_____

_____

_____

_____

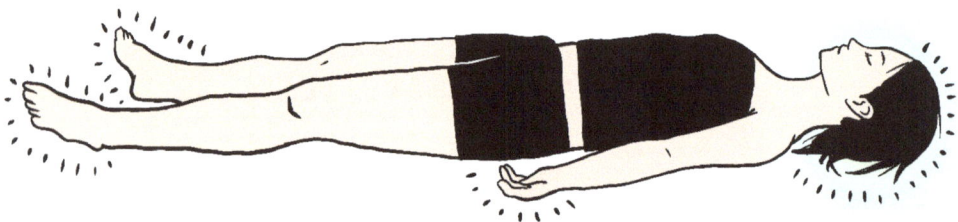

SAVASANA POSE

Final resting pose –
Rejuvenate as you find peace in the stillness

Awaken your spirit, channel mental energy inward,
Slow brainwaves to discover your creativity...
A rejuvenation of mind, body, and spirit
To master life's external influences...
Allow exploration from the inside-out...

SAVASANA POSE:
I FEEL THE REJUVENATION...

_____

_____

_____

_____

_____

_____

_____

_____

_____

_____

_____

_____

_____

NAMASTE

"The light in me honors the light in you."

Love conquers...

NAMASTE: *I* SEE THE LIGHT...

_____
_____
_____
_____
_____
_____
_____
_____
_____
_____
_____
_____
_____
_____
_____
_____
_____
_____
_____

CHAKRAS

The Seven Wheels of Energy

ROOT (Red)
Passion, Survival, Safety

SACRAL (Orange)
Creativity, Emotional, and Sexual Energy

SOLAR PLEXUS (Yellow)
Intellect, Personal Power

HEART (Green)
Love, Compassion

THROAT (Blue)
Serenity, Self-Expression

THIRD EYE (Indigo)
Inner Wisdom

CROWN (Deep Purple)
Transcendence, Spirituality

Balance these vortexes of energy

For emotional and physical harmony...

CHAKRAS: *I feel the sensation...*

INHALE + EXHALE + REFRESH +
BLOOM + CALM

STILLNESS + CHANGE + BE PRESENT +
RENEW + REJUVENATE

RELAX + OCEAN BREEZE + SUN +
MOON + STARS

VISION BOARD

Create your life.
Place your inner desires
on your personal vision board.
Words, photos, drawings…
Look at it every day.
Believe what is within will
manifest without.

STRENGTH + JOY + TRANQUILITY +
MEDITATION + LAUGHTER

**Use this page to write down ideas
and plan a design for your vision board.**

_____

_____

_____

_____

_____

_____

_____

_____

_____

_____

_____

_____

_____

_____

_____

_____

_____

_____

_____

_____

_____

_____

_____

_____

_____

SANDRA K

CERTIFIED HOT YOGA INSTRUCTOR, ACTRESS, AND TALK SHOW HOST, Sandra's love for life, family, the art of the yoga practice, appreciating the beauty of Mother Nature, the greater outdoors, and the value of freedom have inspired this book.

Sandra has enjoyed teaching yoga privately, in groups, at places of worship, and on the beach. She loves to share the overwhelming mental and physical benefits of the yoga practice with all. Sandra has donated her time to the North Shore Child and Family Guidance Center that is devoted to restoring and strengthening the emotional well-being of children and their families.

Following a long, successful career as an executive in the garment center, Sandra enjoyed marketing her products live on QVC National Television. She has developed a one-woman show series, *Exit Strategy: An Evening with Sandra K*, which has been performed at the Southampton Cultural Center.

Sandra hosts *Cafe* ☕ *with Sandra K* on LTV-EH, East Hampton public access television station. She attended the American Academy of Dramatic Arts and is a resident of Water Mill, N.Y.

JOANNE DE SIMONE

WRITER, FILM HISTORIAN, AWARD-WINNING PLAYWRIGHT, POET, AND FORMER FILM COLUMNIST for *Fire Island News*, Joanne's work has been featured in various publications and film journals. Her plays have been produced in NYC festivals, and many of them may be viewed on YouTube. Joanne's books are available in bookstores and online. She currently hosts *Notes & Notions from The Writing Desk* on East Hampton's LTV-EH. She is a "script/prose/poetry doctor" for fellow writers.

Joanne recently launched St. Rita & Archangel Metatron Arts League, a non-profit organization to inspire and encourage tweens and teens to follow their artistic endeavors. To learn more, visit stramal.com.

ANNETTE LEE

DESIGNER AND ILLUSTRATOR, Annette has been drawing her whole life and attended the School of Visual Arts for Graphic Design and Advertising. She currently works at Penguin Random House where she designs ads and promotions for books, which include short videos, posters, social media posts, and more. She is also studying film and animation in hopes of expanding her skill set in digital art and still loves to draw in her spare time.

www.ingramcontent.com/pod-product-compliance
Lightning Source LLC
Chambersburg PA
CBHW051238090426
42742CB00001B/17